Food That Anchors
Recipes for People On the Go

Ellen C Lee

Food That Anchors
Recipes for People On the Go

Ellen C Lee

Ramen Started It All

The First Meal I Made: Fancy Ramen

My sister was the first role model in my life. There was a ten year age gap and we didn't grow up under the same roof, but I always admired her wisdom, grace, poise, and strength. She was always away at school in another city, so our time together was limited, but I cherished it. The few weekends she came home, she taught me interesting skills like wrapping gifts with elaborate folds, and cooking fancy ramen.

The first hot meal I made was the Tung I brand ramen with soup on the side. It was considered "fancy" because the process was more complicated than dropping everything in hot water. My sister showed me how to blanch the ramen, pulling out just the noodles to toss together with the flavor oil. Then, we made the soup separately by ladling hot water into a bowl to dissolve the dry seasoning in it.

At age seven, I felt like a chef.

Food As An Anchor

Meal times were a constant in my volatile upbringing. Lunch at noon and dinner at six o'clock. Unless someone was being punished, it was mandatory to show up to eat at the dining table. There was no excusing yourself from the table.

Today I share about this militant meal schedule from the vantage point of having worked through the trauma of my childhood.

Our dining table was once a battlefield, our version of the Cold War. My dad was a ticking time bomb, set off by seemingly trivial things - food gone cold, not enough vegetables, chicken too dry, etc. We ate in the silence between blowouts, anxiously waiting for the other shoe to drop.

The decision to include my past is not an attempt to relive it. Rather, I want to highlight the healing journey God took me through.

Though the execution of my upbringing was traumatic, my parents did their best in raising us. They grew up with a scarcity of parental guidance and resources. They both were the oldest child in their family and were forced to assume the responsibility of taking care of everyone else.

Overcoming trauma is not as simple as doing the opposite of what you have experienced. I know that now and am so grateful for the years of counseling and the supportive community I have, but those resources were not available in my parents' generation.

Post healing, beyond the trauma, now I can see what I had around meal times is rare in today's society; balanced meals cooked from fresh ingredients. Meals were eaten on a regular schedule, and we always ate together as a family. Somehow, the busyness of after school activities, my parents' business, and phone calls, everything ceased around meal times.

That level of consistency was actually an anchor that held our family together.

No matter the level of tension, we always ate together. Food connected our family, and through the years I noticed the commonality of people being bonded through meals.

Food is a universal language that bypasses tension or silence. It bridges the chasm of differences.

The older I get, the less time I seem to have. More than ever food anchors me in relationships, and helps me to stay connected with the community. Through years of countless relocations due to schools and jobs, dining out or hosting dinner parties with friends became an outlet for me to balance hustle with humanity.

There were years when being busy was my way to avoid building deep relationships. In those times, it was easier to bury myself in work and fill my social calendar with events than to confront the absence of quality relationships. Quantity over quality was my guiding life principle then. Those were dark times.

God never intended for us to be incubated by busyness resulting in isolation (sometimes known as "independence"), yet, how many of us eat while surfing our social media accounts whether dining solo or otherwise? How many times do we witness a sea of blue screen-lit faces at restaurants? How many of us compromise nutrition and health for the convenience of microwave dinner or drive-thrus? We can honor food as an anchor connecting us to ourselves and to others by cooking delicious meals that feed our souls and the relationships around us.

About Me

Growing up in the food-centric culture of Taiwan, we were surrounded by the best natural resources and agricultural abundance. Fruits were exotic and ripe. The varieties of vegetables were countless. Seafood was plentiful, and there seemed to be more restaurants or hawker stalls than any other type of business. Food was the ubiquitous connector. When you visit relatives, regardless of the hour of the day, you eat. When you want to thank someone or build a business connection, you give a box of premium fruits as a gift. When you want an adventure, you visit the night market to eat from stall to stall. The love for food ran in my family. We each have a love for specific foods, but in general, there was no food we avoided. When I immigrated to the U.S., due to the limited variety of Asian food at the time, if we craved a dish, we learned to cook it. That was when my palette was trained to identify flavors and to create different flavor profiles.

As a professional organizer, I like all things efficient! I especially love creating processes that remove redundancy for the sake of improving efficiency. It was the realization of this passion and having ruled out OCD that I founded *Ellen C Lee Organizer*. My mission now is to create order to eliminate chaos, so you can see beyond the clutter to live your authentic life. Time is valuable, and everything we commit to doing deserves our full attention; however, overcommitment can often lead to busyness and unmanaged busyness can become overwhelming.

In the same vein that *Ellen C Lee Organizer* is founded to restore the lost efficiency and peace in your homes, I have married that skillset with my passion for food. Every recipe in this book can be made in 60 minutes or less! In cooking, the most efficient way may not be the most delicious or nutritious (i.e. frozen dinner), so all of the recipes in this cookbook are designed to strike that delicate balance of efficiency and taste. Understanding the need to be efficient without robbing you of the experience to have an orgasmic culinary experience gave birth to this cookbook. If you have ever had that "OMG, this is the best thing I've ever put in my mouth" experience, you know what I am talking about.

My hope is that this cookbook will show you a way to overcome the busyness preventing you from cooking and eating well. May you be inspired to fuel yourself differently upon learning cooking does not always equate to time sacrifice. With proper planning, cooking can be efficient, fun, and perhaps bring out the creative side in you! Maybe you are new to the kitchen, or have been burned in the past (no pun intended). I hope you will see your time in the kitchen differently, become re-acquainted with the joy of cooking; and maybe, it will become a skillset to create family recipes to pass on for generations to come!

The Journey I Didn't Have Time For...

In 2018, I met an extraordinary Declutter Coach, Yvette, with whom I partnered to start Organize Your Busy Life. We run in-person workshops that teach people ways to organize and overcome the busyness of each season. The workshops were sponsored by services we hand selected that provide added values to eliminate stress.

Meal prep was an obvious service to invest in to minimize stress. In one workshop, we could not find an available meal prep service to sponsor us, so at the last minute I decided to prepare the lunch myself. The idea was to keep it simple, so I could focus on the workshop and not on serving food. We served the Power Rolled Sandwich, the Fresh Fig & Goat Cheese Arugula, and the Pesto Quinoa Salad. To our surprise, in post workshop testimonial videos, an overwhelming majority commented on how good the food was, specifically that it did not weigh them down or lead them to the usual post lunch afternoon lull.

There was a moment after that workshop when I heard God nudge me with, "Don't be selfish, share your gift and write a cookbook." I responded to that divine download with a very human dismissal, "I don't have time for that," "it's too expensive to write a cookbook," "people don't buy cookbooks anymore." Yet, three years later, that nudge persisted. In 2021, I put ink to paper, took photos of the food I cooked, shared them on social media, and hired professionals for every step of making a cookbook. And here we are!

Contents

SAUCES, DRESSINGS & MARINADES	10
POWER BITES	34
BREAKFAST	42
WEEKDAYS	44
WEEKENDS	58
LUNCH	72
SALADS	74
HANDHELDS	84
THREE STUFFED AMIGOS	92
TACOS	100
DINNER	126
MAIN DISHES	128
VEGAN BOWLS	140
CLOSING	160

Sauces, Dressings & Marinades

"An ounce of sauce covers a multitude of sins."
– Anthony Bourdain

My mom is a human flavor detector. One of my favorite questions to ask when we dine out is, "What do you taste in this sauce?" She can break down the flavor profile and deduce the ingredients in the sauce. If we like the dish, she can recreate it at home. You can not tell the difference.

Sauces are a game changer. They can take a dish from good to amazing in a split second. This section is your secret weapon to efficient cooking. By marinating your protein before cooking it, adding the sauces to a bowl of grains and roasted vegetables, or dressing up a salad, no flavors are omitted for the sake of efficiency.

DAIRY FREE PESTO

CASHEW SOUR CREAM

PONZU CREAM

SAGE TAHINI SAUCE

GARLIC TAHINI SAUCE

GINGER SCALLION HOT OIL

TERIYAKI SAUCE

TURMERIC MISO DRESSING

GARLIC DIJON MAPLE DRESSING

SESAME PEANUT SAUCE

BASIL DRESSING

CHINESE CHICKEN SALAD DRESSING

LEMONY DRESSING

MISO GLAZE MARINADE

CHUNKY SALSA

SAUCES, DRESSINGS & MARINADES

MEDITERRANEAN SALAD

Dairy Free Pesto

This pesto is versatile and packs a lot of flavor. You won't even miss the cheese! You can toss it with spaghetti squash for a vegan pasta, spoon it on top of cubed tofu and tomatoes for a vegan caprese salad, or simply use as you would any pesto.

Yields: 8 oz · Total Time: 10 min

Ingredients

3 cloves of garlic
1 1/2 c basil
1 1/2 c cilantro
2 tbsp sunflower seeds

1/2 c extra virgin olive oil
1 tsp lemon juice
3/4 tsp salt

Method

1. Add all ingredients excluding olive oil into the food processor.
2. Slowly drizzle in olive oil as you process.
3. Add more olive oil as needed to reach the smooth, desired consistency.

Cashew Sour Cream

Top bowls with this cream for added protein, or use as you would a traditional sour cream on tacos, chili, nachos and more.

Yields: 16 oz · Total Time: 5 min + 20 min (or overnight) to soak cashews

Ingredients

2 c raw unsalted cashews
1/2 c lemon juice
1/2 c apple cider vinegar
1/2 c water

Method

1. Soak cashews in filtered water overnight OR in boiling water for 20 minutes.
2. Combine all ingredients in Vitamix and blend to emulsify.

Chunky Salsa

Yields: 12-16 oz · Total Time: 15 min

Ingredients

2 medium size tomatoes
1 serrano chili
1/4 c diced onion
1/4 c chopped cilantro
Juice of 1/2 of a lemon
Salt & pepper to taste

Seasonal Variations, add one of the following:

1/2 c gooseberries
1/2 c diced mango
1/2 c diced pineapple

Method

1. Dice tomatoes into small chunks.
2. Roughly chop the cilantro.
3. Finely dice the onions and serrano chili. If you want it spicier, include the seeds. Otherwise, remove the seeds.
4. Mix all ingredients together with lemon juice, salt, and pepper.
5. If you like a smooth salsa, pulse tomatoes in a Vitamix or food processor until the desired smoothness.

Ponzu Cream

This super fast, simple cream packs so much flavor! We use vegan mayo for its lighter consistency, but it does not make this sauce vegan! It serves as a great condiment to drizzle on roasted vegetables or combine with cooked lentils or farro for a tasty grain salad.

Yields: 8 oz · Total Time: 5 min

Ingredients

1 c vegan mayo
2 tbsp sesame oil
4 tbsp ponzu
4 tbsp ginger root

Method

1. Roughly chop ginger root with skin on.
2. Combine all ingredients into a Vitamix personal cup, and blend using the personal cup adapter. If you don't have the Vitamix personal cup adapter, double the recipe till the volume reaches the minimum level of the blender pitcher.

Optional Method

1. Use a microplane to grate the fresh ginger root.
2. Stir together all the ingredients to mix well.

Sage Tahini Sauce

A super easy to make sauce that brings life to any roasted vegetable. Great on bowls.

Yields: 10 oz · Total Time: 10 min

Ingredients

1 1/4 c tahini
1/4 c hot water (more as needed)
3/4 c lemon juice

6 cloves of garlic
3/4 c fresh sage
Salt to taste

Method

1. Boil water.
2. Blend all together in Vitamix. Add hot water as needed to thin out to a paint-like consistency.

Garlic Tahini Sauce

Simple, yet packs a lot of flavor. Great on bowls.

Yields: 6 oz · Total Time: 10 min

Ingredients

1/2 c tahini
2 tbsp hot water (more as needed)
2 tbsp olive oil

1 tbsp dark soy sauce or tamari
4 cloves of garlic, pressed

Method

1. Boil water.
2. In a small mixing bowl, combine tahini with olive oil and hot water. Whisk until a paint-like consistency.
3. Smash the garlic cloves to separate them from their skin, then using a garlic press, press into the bowl.
4. Add soy sauce or tamari, whisk well.

Ginger Scallion Hot Oil

Serve over pork tenderloins, steamed fish, or poached chicken.

Yields: 8 oz · Total Time: 10 min

Ingredients

1/3 c chopped ginger root
1 c chopped scallions
1/3 c dark sesame oil

1/3 c olive oil
1 tsp salt

Method

1. Combine the scallions and ginger in a food processor, and blend until a paste-like consistency. Add 1 tbsp water if needed. Set aside in a glass bowl.
2. Heat the oil combination on high until the oil bubbles when you sprinkle with water.
3. Pour the hot oil into the scallions and ginger mixture, stir at the same time until they are well combined.

Caution: oil may splatter, as hot oil comes in contact with water in the scallions ginger mixture.

Teriyaki Sauce

Yields: 8 oz · Total Time: 18 min

Ingredients

2 tbsp grated ginger root
1/2 c soy sauce
1/4 c honey

1/4 c water
3 tbsp sugar

Method

1. Combine grated ginger, water, honey, sugar in a small pot (or a saute pan), place on the stove on medium heat, whisk to dissolve the sugar and honey.
2. Add soy sauce, then turn heat to medium-high, stirring occasionally for 10-15 minutes until sauce thickens.
3. Dip the back of the spoon into the sauce, then run your finger through, it should leave a trail that does not fill in.
4. If you want it thicker, allow the sauce to bubble gently around the edges for a few more minutes.

Turmeric Miso Dressing

Make a bottle of this and store in the fridge for up to a month! Great on bowls.

Yields: 16 oz · Total Time: 10 min

Ingredients

2 tbsp white miso
1 c hot water
1/3 c white wine vinegar

1/2 c sesame oil
1/2 c olive oil
2 tsp turmeric powder

Method

1. Boil water.
2. Dissolve miso paste with enough hot water until a smooth, paint-like consistency.
3. Whisk in turmeric into the miso mixture.
4. Whisk the remaining ingredients together with the miso mixture.
5. Transfer to a shaker bottle or a mason jar for storage.

Garlic Dijon Maple Dressing

Yields: 4 oz · Total Time: 5 min

Ingredients

2 cloves of garlic, pressed
1 tsp dijon mustard
1 tbsp maple syrup
1 tbsp white wine vinegar
3 tbsp olive oil

Method

1. Smash the garlic cloves to separate them from their skin, then using a garlic press, press into a small bowl.
2. Add the rest of the ingredients, whisk by hand.

Sesame Peanut Sauce

Yields: 8 oz · Total Time: 10 min

Ingredients

4 tbsp organic creamy peanut butter
3/4 c hot water (more as needed)
1 tbsp dark sesame oil
1 tbsp light soy sauce
1 tsp grated ginger root

Method

1. Boil water.
2. In a small mixing bowl, whisk peanut butter with a little hot water till it thins out.
3. Use a microplane to grate the ginger root with skin on.
4. Add the rest of the ingredients. Whisk to combine well.
5. Add more hot water, if needed to reach a paint-like consistency.

SAUCES, DRESSINGS & MARINADES

Basil Dressing

Pair this with the **Mediterranean Salad** in the Lunch section. It's great on other salads too!

Yields: 10 oz · Total Time: 4 min

Ingredients

3 cloves of garlic
2 c sweet basil
1 c extra virgin olive oil
1 tbsp honey
1/4 c lemon juice
Zest of half of a lemon

Method

1. Combine all ingredients in a blender and blend until well incorporated.

Chinese Chicken Salad Dressing

Pairs with the **Crispy Garlic Chicken Salad** in the Lunch section. A classic Asian flavor profile.

Yields: 6 oz · Total Time: 6 min

Ingredients

2 tbsp sesame oil
1/4 c olive oil
2 tbsp rice wine vinegar
Juice of half of an orange
Salt & pepper to taste

Method

1. In a large mixing bowl whisk together the ingredients until well incorporated.

Lemony Dressing

Pair this with the **Fresh Figs & Goat Cheese Arugula Salad** in the Lunch section. It's a refreshing dressing for summertime salads.

Yields: 6 oz · Total Time: 4 min

Ingredients

2 tbsp apple cider vinegar
4 tbsp extra virgin olive oil
1 tsp honey
Zest of 1 lemon
Salt to taste

Method

1. In a large mixing bowl whisk together the ingredients for the dressing..

CRISPY GARLIC CHINESE CHICKEN SALAD

Miso Glaze Marinade

Perfect for marinating cod, leave the cod overnight in the fridge for flavor to sufficiently permeate. The total time is still less than 60 minutes to make the marinade and roast the fish!

Yields: 8 oz · Total Time: 18 min

Ingredients

1/2 c white miso paste
1/2 c mirin

1/2 c sake
4 tbsp sugar

Method

1. Combine 1/2 c mirin, 1/2 c sake, 4 tbsp sugar in a sauce pot and boil for 20 sec. to cook off the alcohol. Remove from heat.
2. Whisk in 1/2 c white miso paste until smooth.

Power Bites

"Keep your friends close, and your snacks closer."
– Unknown

If you are a grazer like me, or are constantly on the go, please pack a snack to sustain you through the day. Let these simple recipes be fuel to you and/or your little ones.

LEMON CRANBERRY

GINGER CARROT

MEXICAN "HOT CHOCOLATE"

MEXICAN "HOT CHOCOLATE" POWER BITES

Lemon Cranberry

These power bites are great bite-sized poppers you can make ahead of time and store in the freezer for up to a month.

Makes: 30 balls · Total Time: 30 min

Ingredients

1 c dried cranberries
1 c roasted unsalted almonds
2 c shredded coconut, set aside 1 cup
2 tbsp toasted flax seeds
1 c unsalted almond butter

1/2 c honey
A dash of salt
3 drops doTERRA lemon essential oil or 4 tbsp fresh lemon juice

Method

1. Combine all ingredients in a food processor, mix well. There may be small chunks of crane berries, that's totally fine.
2. Use a 1" melon baller to scoop up the mixture.
3. Roll each ball in the remaining shredded coconut.
4. Place rolled power bites in a parchment paper lined, freezer safe container, store in the freezer until ready to eat. Texture is softer at room temperature.

Pro Tip: Put the mixture in the freezer until consistency becomes more dense before portioning.

Ginger Carrot

Not to be confused with cake pops, this carrot cake in ball form will satisfy any sweet tooth and give you a boost in energy!

Makes: 30 balls · Total Time: 35 min

Ingredients

1 c rolled oats
3/4 c shredded carrots
2 c unsweetened shredded coconut, set aside 1 cup
2 c tightly packed pitted dates

1 tsp cinnamon
1 tsp ground ginger
1/4 tsp salt
1 tbsp water (more as needed)

Method

1. Shred 1-2 medium sized carrots in the food processor first. Measure out 3/4 c.
2. Pulse the oats separately to break them down. Then add all remaining ingredients, except the water, and process until consistency is like wet sand. Pro Tip: roughly chop the dates first to help the food processor break down their dense consistency.
3. Add the water, if necessary. Sometimes the carrots provide enough liquid for the right consistency of wet sand.
4. Use a small 1" melon baller or a tablespoon to portion out each ball. Then roll by hand. And lightly roll each ball in a bowl of shredded coconut. If you like your energy bites uncoated, omit rolling each ball in shredded coconut.
5. Line the balls on a parchment paper lined sheet pan. Store in the fridge until ready to serve.

Mexican "Hot Chocolate"

It looks like a truffle, tastes like a truffle, and fuels you like a meal! Don't let their unassuming monotone appearance fool you. These bites are sweet and creamy up front, but pack a subtle heat that creeps up. If you're not a fan of spicy, simply skip the cayenne pepper.

Makes: 20 balls · Total Time: 25 min

Ingredients

1 1/2 c rolled oats
1/4 c unsweetened shredded coconut
1/4 cup chia seeds
1/4 c spicy bourbon honey (or use regular honey and add another 1/4 tsp cayenne pepper)

1 c almond butter
10 large pitted dates
1/4 c cacao powder
1/4 tsp cayenne pepper
1 tsp cinnamon
1 tsp vanilla extract

Method

1. Break up the oats first in a food processor.
2. Chop the dates into smaller chunks, add to the food processor with the rest of the ingredients.
3. Pulse until all ingredients are combined, a wet sand consistency.
4. Scoop with a 1" melon baller or a 1/2 tbsp measuring spoon and roll by hand.
5. Line the balls on a parchment paper lined sheet pan. Store in the fridge until ready to consume.

Breakfast

"A meal without wine is called breakfast."
– Me

Breakfast took on a different rhythm weekdays vs weekends. Growing up, breakfast was not only essential, it was hearty! On the weekdays, I would find either pot stickers, a giant steamed bao filled with cabbage and pork, or a fried egg with a bowl of freshly made hot soy milk waiting for us on the dining table. Except on those weekdays instead of soy milk, the food would be paired with a hot cup of milk made from powder, lumps of undissolved powder still floating in it. Those undissolved lumps signified the hurriedness of weekday breakfasts.

Weekends, however, were a treat. They would range from red bean paste filled bread to a pastry filled with salty egg yolks. Really, more like desserts in disguise as weekend breakfasts. The departure from the hearty weekday breakfasts signified the more relaxed nature of weekends. During the summertime though, when I would go visit and stay with my grandmother, breakfast would be a giant hamburger, almost 6 inches, distinct layers of patty, lettuce, onions, and tomatoes sandwiched between sesame studded buns.

The memory of how breakfast set the tone for the day has conditioned me to approach this first meal with intention.

WEEKDAYS

WEEKENDS

BREAKFAST

Breakfast: Weekdays

Whether you enjoy a power breakfast, or intermittent fast till lunch as your first meal, overnight oats are the perfect weekday breakfast items designed to give you that energy lift without weighing you down.

You can make a variety of bases ahead of time, and store them in the fridge. When you are ready to consume, either as breakfast or a snack, whether at home or as a grab-n-go option, just pack them in individual serving mason jars and add the toppings suggested before serving. It's easy, nutritious, and versatile! I hope these combinations inspire you to create your own flavor combinations!

OVERNIGHT OATS:

BASES & TOPPINGS

BREAKFAST: WEEKDAYS

Bases

BERRIES CINNAMON CHOCOLATE

Banana Base

Makes 5 servings | Total Time 8 min

Ingredients

2 1/2 c rolled oats
1 tbsp chia seeds
3 c almond milk
2 ripe bananas
3 tbsp maple syrup
1/2 tbsp vanilla extract

Method

1. In a large bowl, mash the bananas using a fork. Whisk in the rest of the ingredients.
2. Divide into 5 - 16 oz. mason jars, 1 for each weekday. Store in the fridge.
3. Add more almond milk if needed for desired consistency. Before serving, add the toppings suggested in the Toppings section.

Chocolate Lovers Base

Makes 5 servings | Total Time 8 min

Ingredients

2 1/2 c rolled oats
1 tbsp chia seeds
1 1/2 c almond milk
1 1/2 c coconut milk (full fat from a can)
1/4 c maple syrup
1/2 tbsp vanilla extract
1/3 c unsweetened cocoa powder

Method

1. Blend together almond milk, coconut milk, and cacao powder.
2. Add remaining ingredients to a large mixing bowl, whisk together by hand.
3. Divide into 5 - 16 oz. mason jars, 1 for each weekday. Store in the fridge for up to a week.
4. Add more almond milk if needed for desired consistency. Before serving, add the toppings suggested in the Toppings section.

Cinnamon Base

Makes 5 servings | Total Time 8 min

Ingredients

2 1/2 c rolled oats
1 tbsp chia seeds
2 1/2 c almond milk
3 tbsp maple syrup
1/2 tbsp vanilla extract
1/2 tbsp cinnamon
A pinch of Himalayan pink salt

Method

1. Whisk together cinnamon, maple syrup, vanilla extract, and almond milk in a large mixing bowl.
2. Add remaining ingredients. Stir until oats and chia seeds are well coated.
3. Divide into 5 - 16 oz. mason jars, 1 for each weekday. Store in the fridge.
4. Add more almond milk if needed for desired consistency. Before serving, add the toppings suggested in the Toppings section.

Coconut Base

Makes 5 servings | Total Time 8 min

Ingredients

2 1/2 c rolled oats
1 tbsp chia seeds
3 c coconut milk (full fat from a can)
Almond milk (as needed)
1/4 c maple syrup
1/2 tbsp vanilla extract

Method

1. Whisk together coconut milk, maple syrup, and vanilla extract in a large mixing bowl until the fat and liquid are combined.
2. Add remaining ingredients. Stir until oats and chia seeds are well coated.
3. Divide into 5 - 16 oz. mason jars, 1 for each weekday. Store in the fridge.
4. Add more almond milk if needed for desired consistency. Before serving, add the toppings suggested in the Toppings section.

Berries Base

Makes 5 servings | Total Time 8 min

Ingredients

2 1/2 c rolled oats
1 tbsp chia seeds
2 1/2 c almond milk

3 c frozen mixed berries
1/4 c maple syrup
1/2 tbsp vanilla extract

Method

1. Blend the berries with almond milk.
2. Combine remaining ingredients in a large mixing bowl.
3. Divide into 5 - 16 oz. mason jars, 1 for each weekday. Store in the fridge.
4. Before serving, add more almond milk if needed for desired consistency, then add the toppings suggested in the Toppings section.

Toppings

ALMOST ELVIS

TROPICAL PARADISE

CLASSIC STRAWBERRY BANANA

BAKED APPLE PIE

Almost Elvis

Banana Base + Toppings:

A dollop of peanut butter
Flax seeds
Drizzle honey on top

Classic Strawberry Banana

Banana Base + Toppings:

Fresh strawberries, sliced
Flax seeds
Sliced almonds

PB & J

Berries Base + Toppings:

A dollop of peanut butter
Fresh strawberries, sliced
Flax seeds

Almond Joy

Coconut Base + Toppings:

Coconut chips
Cacao nibs
A dollop of almond butter

BREAKFAST: OVERNIGHT OATS TOPPINGS

ALMOST ELVIS

CLASSIC STRAWBERRY BANANA

PB&J

ALMOND JOY

BAKED APPLE PIE

CHOCOLATE CHERRY CORDIALS

TROPICAL PARADISE

CHOCOLATE COVERED BANANAS

Baked Apple Pie

Cinnamon Base + Toppings:

Fresh apples diced
Flax seeds
A dollop of almond butter

Chocolate Cherry Cordials

Chocolate Lovers Base + Toppings:

Frozen bing cherries, thawed
Cacao nibs
Sliced almonds

Tropical Paradise

Berries Base + Toppings:

Fresh mangos or pineapples
Shredded unsweetened coconut
Hemp seeds

Chocolate Covered Bananas

Banana Base + Toppings:

Sliced bananas
Cocoa nibs
A dollop of almond butter

Breakfast: Weekends

The weekend breakfast items are designed to give you permission to slow down and connect with friends and loved ones. Making great food is fun and making it for people you love is a privilege. I hope these recipes inspire you to invite some friends over. Do not be shy to ask them to bring the bubbly!

GARLIC TARTS

STRAWBERRY BACON TOASTS

POMEGRANATE CREAM CHEESE TOAST

AVOCADO TOAST BAR

SPICY TOMATO EGGS

EGG & SAUSAGE CUPS

SWEET POTATOES RICE PORRIDGE

POMEGRANATE CREAM CHEESE TOAST

BREAKFAST: WEEKENDS

Garlic Tarts

This recipe is pushing the 60 minute standard, but it's so worth the extra 10 minutes. The trick here is to stagger the steps, prep while the garlic roasts in the oven. Plus cleaning up is easy!

Makes: 12 tarts · Total Time: 53 min + time to soften cream cheese

Ingredients

5 bulbs of garlic, roasted
8 oz. cream cheese
3 tsp fresh thyme
1 1/2 tsp salt
1 tsp white pepper

1 can of crescent roll dough (any brand)
2 tbsp honey
1/4 c chives
1/4 c roasted pecans

Method

1. Leave cream cheese at room temperature to soften.
2. Roast garlic:
   - Cut off the heads of the garlic bulbs, enough to expose the garlic inside. Wrap the entire bulb in a foil, drizzle olive oil, salt and peper before sealing into a pouch.
   - Roast garlic pouches in a 400 degree oven for 40 minutes. Garlic will become soft and creamy. Simply squeeze them out of bulbs into a bowl. Set aside.
   - Lower the temperature of the oven to 375 degrees.
3. While the garlic is roasting, separate and chop thyme and chives. Roll the dough from the can to cut into 12 squares.
4. Grease a muffin tin with butter, lay each dough square inside the hole with edges sticking out.
5. Combine room temperature cream cheese and roasted garlic, thyme, salt and white pepper using a masher.
6. Fill each muffin hole with cream cheese mixture 3/4 way to the top.
7. Bake in the oven for 11-13 minutes.
8. Drizzle the roasted tarts with honey and sprinkle chopped chives and pecan pieces.

Strawberry Bacon Toast

This simple, seasonal inspired toast is heartier than it sounds. The sweetness from fresh juicy strawberries and the crunchy salty bacon paired with the creamy, tangy goat cheese combination is sure to satiate, and the presentation is crowd pleasing too! Instead of strawberries, you can also use blackberries.

Serves: 6-8 people · Total Time: 35 min + time to soften goat cheese

Ingredients

8 oz. log of goat cheese
1 pack 12 oz. bacon (regular thickness)
16 oz. fresh strawberries
1.75 oz. microgreens

1 loaf of french bread
1/3 c extra virgin olive oil
3 tbsp honey
Salt & pepper to taste

Method

1. Leave goat cheese at room temperature to soften.
2. Preheat the oven to 400 degrees. Line bacon on a baking rack on top of a baking sheet, or just a parchment lined baking sheet. Bake for 15-20 minutes depending on the thickness of bacon.
3. While bacon is cooking, slice the french bread into 1/2 inch thickness and toast them in a second oven, at 350 degrees for 10 minutes, flip half way.
4. If working with a single oven, move on to step 5 while waiting for bacon to cook.
5. Mix softened goat cheese with olive oil until smooth. I find a fork handy for this job!
6. When toasts are done, butter and smear a generous layer.
7. Add a handful of microgreens on top of goat cheese. Add salt and pepper.
8. Crumble bacon into large chunks, sprinkle on the microgreens, and top with slices of strawberries. To avoid toppings falling, insert the strawberry slices in the crevices of the microgreens.
9. Drizzle honey and extra virgin olive oil, crack fresh black pepper as the final touch.

Pomegranate Cream Cheese Toast

Inspired by colors of the fall and winter seasons— the time of the year when we transition from Thanksgiving to Christmas. This simple toast will complement any brunch or serve as an afternoon snack. It's easy, colorful, and comforting.

Serves: 6-8 people · Total Time: 20 min + time to soften cream cheese

Ingredients

1 loaf of pumpkin brioche bread (see substitution in Method)
2 c fresh pomegranate arils
2 tbsp raspberry jam
8 oz. cream cheese, room temperature
1 c fresh mint

Method

1. Toast and butter sliced pumpkin brioche bread. If you can't find these seasonal pumpkin brioche bread at Trader Joe's, use any brioche bread and slice to 1 inch thickness, sprinkle with some cinnamon and pumpkin pie spice after toasting and buttering.
2. Add a generous layer of cream cheese.
3. Dollop raspberry jam randomly on the cream cheese, swirl them around with a knife.
4. Top with fresh pomegranate arils and sprinkle some torn mint.

Pro Tip: Break open a pomegranate over a large bowl of water, remove the outer peel, then break the arils into the bowl of water. Any small pieces of peel will float to the top of the water, just skim them then drain the water, leaving just the arils.

Avocado Toast Bar

For those with a diverse palette, this is a fun idea for brunch to gather friends who like different types of food. (Well, they have to agree on liking avocados!) It is a highly customizable dish. Depending on the size of your party, you can even include fried eggs and crumbled bacon. Have fun and create additional toppings based on your preference.

Serves: 9-12 people · Total Time: 20 min

Ingredients

Half of a loaf of a large french bread
5 large ripe avocados
2 tbsp extra virgin olive oil
1 tbsp garlic powder
Zest of a large lemon
Salt & pepper to taste

Toppings (set these out buffet style)

1 c goat cheese, crumbled
1 c cherry tomatoes, quartered
Sunflower seeds
Balsamic glaze
Extra virgin olive oil
Red pepper chili flakes
Furikake (Japanese seaweed seasoning)

Method

1. Preheat the oven to 350 degrees.
2. Smash the avocados and mix with garlic powder, salt, and pepper.
3. Slice the french bread at 1/2 inch thickness, butter, line on a baking sheet, and toast for about 10 minutes, flip half way.
4. Toss the quartered tomatoes in olive oil, lemon zest, salt, and pepper.
5. Lay out all toppings separately, buffet style.

Egg & Sausage Cups

Make this classic dish on the weekends to enjoy all week as a grab-n-go breakfast or an anytime paleo snack! It can be made ahead of time and stored in the freezer for up to 2 weeks.

Makes: 24 cups · Total Time: 50 min

Ingredients

2 lbs sausage (any kind, I prefer Italian sausages for the fennel flavor profile)
12 eggs
2 c grated or shredded cheese (the cheese of your choice, cheddar, fontina, gouda, or goat are great options)
1/2 c vegetable broth (or half & half)
1 zucchini, diced
1/2 tsp thyme
Salt & pepper to taste

Method

1. Beat eggs and broth (of half & half) together with seasoning.
2. Form sausage cups using a muffin tin, press a thin layer of sausage around the edges and the bottom.
3. Pour egg mixture into the sausage lined muffin tin, 3/4 way to the top.
4. Dice zucchini into 1/2" chunks. (Substitutions: mushrooms, tomatoes, spinach, or bacon).
5. Shred cheese of your choice. I used fontina cheese because that was what I had in the fridge.
6. Fill each egg mixture/ sausage cup with zucchini and cheese. Stir to ensure egg mixture covers the ingredients to avoid uneven cooking.
7. Bake in the oven at 350 degrees for 30 minutes. Eggs will expand when you first pull them out of the oven. Let them cool for a few minutes, then scoop up with a spoon. They should pop out easily.

Spicy Tomato Eggs

This dish is one of my mom's favorites. It is also a traditional country food in Taiwan. In the time my mother was a child when people did not have much meat or seafood to eat, this dish filled the gap. It is subtly tangy from the tomatoes with a hint of sweet from the scallions. While respecting the tradition, I jazzed up this dish with spiciness from the chili and microgreens. Eating it still reminds me of the humble beginning of our heritage.

Serves: 1 person · Total Time: 15 min

Ingredients

2 stalks of scallions
1 tsp chopped serrano chili, seeds removed
1/2 large tomato, diced
2 eggs
1/2 avocado
Handful of microgreens
1 tbsp olive oil
Salt & pepper to taste

Method

1. Chop scallions into 1 inch lengths. Remove the seeds from serrano chili, finely dice them. Chop the tomato into large chunks. Slice avocado at diagonal, leave in the half shell.
2. Whisk eggs, add a splash of water (Pro Tip: this will make the eggs more fluffy).
3. In a small frying pan, heat olive oil at medium-high. Add tomatoes, and stir fry until slightly softened. Add scallions and serrano chili. Season with salt & pepper.
4. Pour egg mixture over the tomatoes and scallions. Season with salt & pepper.
5. As the edge of the egg mixture firms up, use a spatula to push the cooked eggs from the edge toward the center. Tilt the pan to allow the runnier eggs to flow from center to the outer edges. Continue to push eggs to the center until you can fold the whole thing in half. Keep the center slightly runny.
6. Plate the eggs, top with a handful of microgreens, scoop out avocados to fan across the top. Sprinkle salt & pepper on the avocados. Drizzle olive oil over the dish.

Sweet Potato Rice Porridge

This is my comfort food. Growing up, when anyone felt under the weather or experienced stomach issues, porridge would be served. It is nourishing without taxing your digestive system. This version with the sweet potatoes is a classic country dish. Consume it as is or serve with a variety of stir frys.

Serves: 4 people · Total Time: 45 min

Ingredients

1 c short grain white rice
4 c chicken or vegetable broth
2 c sweet potatoes
1/3 c fresh ginger root, julienned

Method

1. Peel and dice the sweet potatoes into large chunks.
2. Rinse the rice until the water is clear.
3. Combine everything in a steamer and cook for 30-40 minutes until the potatoes are soft. If using the traditional stove top method, bring the pot to a boil on high heat. Lower to medium-low heat. Cover. Simmer for 40 minutes.

SWEET POTATO RICE PORRIDGE

Lunch

"Destiny may ride with us today, but there is no reason for it to interfere with lunch."
– Peter the Great

SALADS

HANDHELDS

THREE STUFFED AMIGOS

GREEK STYLE DOUBLE CRUSTED VEGAN PIZZA

Salads

Salads have traditionally been considered a "diet" dish. The underdog reputation is understandable, as many salads are not very exciting or satiating. My hope is you will use this small section as a backdrop to customize your salad by adding proteins, grains, or legumes from the Bowls section to create a salad that satisfies you! You can also leave the recipes as they are to serve as a side dish, or enjoy them on those "diet" days.

CAPRESE TOFU

FRESH FIGS & GOAT CHEESE ARUGULA

PESTO QUINOA

CRISPY GARLIC CHINESE CHICKEN

MEDITERRANEAN

CRISPY GARLIC CHINESE CHICKEN

LUNCH: SALADS

Vegan Caprese Tofu Salad

I love this dish a lot because it can be repurposed into different dishes, epitomizing food efficiency! You can wrap it in a tortilla or jicama wrap and make a taco out of it, warm it up over the stove and serve over brown rice for a vegan bowl, or eat it as an appetizer.

Serves: 4 people · Total Time: 20 min. + 1 hour or overnight for the tofu

Ingredients

- 1 block of firm tofu
- 2 medium tomatoes
- 1/3 c fresh sweet basil, julienned
- 2 stalks of scallions, thinly chopped
- 1/4 c dairy free pesto (see page 13 for recipe)
- 2 tbsp extra virgin olive oil
- 1 tbsp sunflower seeds
- Salt to taste
- Balsamic glaze (any brand)

Method

1. Press out the water in tofu by wrapping the tofu in a kitchen towel. Place the wrapped tofu in a shallow dish, put a baking sheet on top and weigh it down using a heavy item, like a skillet. Leave for an hour or overnight in the fridge.
2. Cube the tofu and toss with pesto until well coated. Let it sit for at least an hour before serving.
3. Toss together the tomatoes, fresh basil, and scallions with olive oil and salt.
4. Add tofu and top with sunflower seeds.
5. Drizzle balsamic glaze as the final touch.

Fresh Figs & Goat Cheese Arugula Salad

This was one of the two recipes that inspired me to write this cookbook. I first made and served this salad in one of the workshops for my organization business. Attendees raved about it in their reviews of the workshop, so here we are. Must give the people what they want!

Serves: 4 people · Total Time: 20 min

Ingredients

7 oz. pre-washed arugula salad
1 c goat cheese, crumbled
1 c fresh figs, diced (use dry figs if fresh figs are not in season)
1 red bell pepper, diced
1 shallot, sliced
2 tbsp flax seeds for topping
Lemony Dressing (see page 31 for recipe)

Method

1. In a large mixing bowl whisk together the ingredients for the dressing.
2. Toss the arugula and shallots in dressing, then top with diced figs, diced bell peppers, goat cheese, and flax seeds.
3. Protein options: hard boiled eggs, canned mackerel in olive oil, rotisserie chicken, sliced chicken breast, or prosciutto.

Vegan Pesto Quinoa Salad

The second recipe that inspired the cookbook you are reading. It is also an understated salad, which fits the criteria of a busy workday lunch – fast to assemble and satisfying. The trick though, is to make the pesto quinoa a day before or use leftover pesto quinoa for more flavor. A great way to use up leftovers and clean out your fridge! If you don't have leftovers, don't fret. The prep time is happening in parallel to cook time, so the total time required is still less than an hour!

Serves: 2 people · Total Time: 30 min

Ingredients

2 c pesto quinoa (see page 144 for recipe)
1 bag of pre-washed spring mix salad
1 avocado, sliced
2 tbsp sliced almonds
Salt & pepper to taste

Pesto Dressing

2 tbsp dairy free pesto (see page 13 for recipe)
1 drop doTERRA oregano essential oil (optional)
2 tbsp extra virgin olive oil
Juice of half of a lemon

Method

1. Cook the quinoa first.
2. Then make the pesto. Combine the two to make pesto quinoa.
3. In a large bowl whisk together pesto with the dressing ingredients for the dressing.
4. Serve pesto quinoa over a bed of spring mix salad tossed in pesto dressing.
5. Top with sliced avocados, sprinkle salt and pepper on the avocados, drizzle with extra virgin olive oil. Sprinkle sliced almonds.

Crispy Garlic Chinese Chicken Salad

There are times when you literally work till the second before you might pass out from hunger. Well, this salad is the solution for those moments. Next time you are at the store and see that warm rotisserie chicken in the hot deli section, think of this recipe. It is a true lifesaver!

Serves 2 people · Total Time 30 min

Ingredients

4 tbsp sesame oil, set half of it aside
5 large cloves of garlic, pressed
1/2 rotisserie chicken, shredded
1 bag of Asian or sesame ginger salad kit
1 avocado
2 mandarin oranges
2 tbsp sunflower seeds
Salt & pepper to taste
Chinese Chicken Salad Dressing (see page 30 for recipe)

Method

1. In a large mixing bowl whisk together the ingredients for the dressing.
2. Warm half of the sesame oil in a pan. Add the pressed garlic and fry until they are golden and crispy.
3. Turn off the heat. Add shredded rotisserie chicken and the remaining sesame oil. Toss to combine garlic and chicken.
4. Assemble the salad kit without the packaged dressing, I recommend the Trader Joe's Asian Sesame Crunch or Costco Asian Salad. This flavor of salad kit is fairly prevalent in mainstream stores now. Sometimes it is called sesame crunch salad.
5. Toss the salad with Chinese Chicken Salad Dressing. Then add sliced avocado, mandarin oranges, and sunflower seeds. Top with crispy garlic chicken.

2 for 1 Meal Idea: Turn this salad into a taco!
1. Crisp up a Folio cheese wrap and form into a taco shell.
2. Assemble the tacos:
   Base - tossed salad with chicken, oranges, and dressing.
   Top - sliced avocados and sunflower seeds.

Mediterranean Salad

This is one of my go-to dishes because I always have these in my fridge. What staples do you have in your fridge?

Serves: 4 people · Total Time: 25 min

Ingredients

7 oz. pre-washed romaine lettuce
7 oz. pre-washed butter lettuce
1/4 red onion, sliced
1/4 c kalamata olives, chopped
1/4 c marinated artichoke hearts, roughly chopped

1/2 c Persian cucumbers, sliced
1/4 c cherry tomatoes, halved
1 avocado, diced
1/2 c goat cheese, crumbled
Salt & pepper to taste
Basil Dressing (see page 30 for recipe)

Method

1. Toss the lettuce and onions with the dressing.
2. Add cucumbers, tomatoes, artichoke hearts, olives, and avocados. Sprinkle salt and pepper. Drizzle more dressing on the ingredients.
3. Top with crumbled goat cheese and protein of choice.
4. Protein options: 1 cup chickpeas (see page 151 for recipe), canned mackerel, roasted chicken breast, or tuna.

Handhelds

The year I met my husband, I quickly realized his obsession with sandwiches, burgers, and pizzas. Since I love my husband, I fed him often. Our marriage has inspired some fun, handheld foods. Time to put your utensils away!

POWER ROLLED SANDWICH

PUMPKIN PATTY MELT

TURKEY TOSTADA

GREEK STYLE DOUBLE CRUSTED VEGAN PIZZA

Power Rolled Sandwich

This is the OG of all recipes, from before I met my husband. It was also one of the recipes that my organization workshop clients raved about in their reviews. The people have spoken so I had to include it in this cookbook!

Serves: 1 person · Total Time: 10 min

Ingredients

1 sheet of lavash bread (white or wheat)
1/4 c hummus
1/2 c power greens
6 slices of turkey breast
1 tbsp flax seeds
Salt & pepper to taste

Method

1. Lay a sheet of lavash bread on parchment paper.
2. Spread a generous layer of hummus on the lavash bread.
3. Sprinkle a layer of flax seeds, followed by turkey breasts, then topped with power greens.
4. Sprinkle on salt and pepper and roll up everything along the long edge while folding the parchment paper on both ends to seal the openings.

Turkey Tostada

This quick, easy dish is perfect for a weekday lunch. It can be easily turned into a vegan and gluten-free option by omitting the ground turkey.

Serves: 2 people · Total Time: 20 min

Ingredients

1 lb. organic ground turkey
2 avocados
4 corn tortilla
1/4 c cilantro, chopped
2 tbsp garlic powder
2 tbsp cumin

2 tbsp paprika
Salt & pepper to taste
1 lemon
Horseradish
Chipotle mayo (*any brand*)
Coconut oil

Method

1. Pan fry the corn tortilla in a shallow pan of coconut oil until crisp, 1-2 min each side.
2. Brown the ground turkey in a separate pan, also in coconut oil. Season with garlic powder, cumin, paprika, salt and pepper.
3. Smear a layer of horseradish on the crisp tortilla, top with ground turkey, and sliced avocados. Squeeze fresh lemon juice over the avocados, followed by a sprinkle of salt and pepper.
4. Drizzle chipotle mayo and garnish with cilantro leaves as the final touch.

Vegan Greek Style Double Crusted Pizza

Serves: 2 people · Total Time: 20 min

Ingredients

2 Greek style pita bread
1 c hummus
2 tbsp extra virgin olive oil, divided into 2 portions
1/3 c pitted kalamata olives, chopped
1/4 c marinated artichoke hearts, chopped
1/4 c red onion, thinly sliced
1 c arugula
1/2 avocado, sliced
1/4 c sunflower seeds
Juice of 1/2 of a lemon
Za'atar seasoning
Salt & pepper to taste

Method

1. Lightly steam pita bread for 3 minutes or until warmed through. If you don't have a steamer, cover the stack of pita bread with a damp paper towel, microwave for 20 seconds.
2. Smear a generous layer of hummus on the top part of a pita, this will be the base layer.
3. Add half of the sliced onions, spread throughout. Drizzle 1 tbsp olive oil. Sprinkle sunflower seeds and artichoke hearts.
4. Put on the second pita, with the top part of the pita facing up. Smear a generous layer of hummus, then add 1 tbsp olive oil.
5. Top with a handful of arugula, remaining onions, and olives.
6. Fan out the avocados on the top layer around the pita bread in a circle. Drizzle lemon juice and sprinkle salt and pepper on the avocados. To finish, sprinkle za'atar seasoning on top.
7. Slice into quarters and serve.

Pumpkin Patty Melt

The month before our wedding, my husband moved to our new neighborhood where he discovered the "Corner Drafthouse", aka his burger distributor. He would order the fig burger often, never tired of it. Since I was not a fan of the price tag of that burger, I decided to make a burger that would rival the fig burger. I'm sharing my victory with you, here is the champ!

Serves: 4 people · Total Time: 20 min

Ingredients

1 lb. grass fed ground beef
4 tbsp Trader Joe's pumpkin spread (seasonal item, can substitute with pumpkin butter)
5 oz. goat's milk brie cheese, sliced (or regular brie cheese)
7 oz. arugula
1 yellow onion, sliced
8 oz. pre-sliced brown bella mushrooms
Lavash bread, cut into squares
1 tsp salt
1 tsp pepper
Olive oil

Method

1. Preheat the oven to 400 degrees. Line the bottom of a 9" x 13" pan with parchment paper.
2. Season beef with salt and pepper, 2 tbsp olive oil. Spread the beef around the pan, corner to corner. Meat will shrink in the pan when it's cooked. Bake in the oven for 10-15 minutes.
3. While the beef is cooking, dry saute sliced mushrooms in a pan until juices flow out, drizzle olive oil, add salt and pepper to taste. Remove the mushrooms from the pan.
4. In the same pan, add 1 tbsp olive oil, sauté sliced onions, add salt and pepper to taste and cook until caramelized.
5. Use a meat thermometer to check on the beef. Once the thermometer reads 160 degrees, top the entire pan with slices of brie to melt. Then cut the meat into the same size squares as the lavash bread, or slightly bigger.
6. **Assemble:** spread a layer of Trader Joe's (or any brand) pumpkin spread on both pieces of lavash bread, top with the beef patty, followed by mushrooms, onions, and finally arugula. Sprinkle salt, pepper, and drizzle some olive oil on the arugula.

   Savory Option: substitute the pumpkin spread with the condiment of your choice.

Three Stuffed Amigos

The following three recipes are crowd pleasers on social media. An overwhelming number of followers "hearted" the photos I posted, and I am certain they were not "hearting" my photography skill. I love the concept of stuffing food into another edible vessel. Similar to tacos and sandwiches, the concept is very efficient and a great way to utilize any leftover ingredients. When you need to put food on the table fast, scour your fridge first to see if you have any ingredients that can become the stuffing. I hope one of these recipes can serve you in those crunch moments.

STUFFED AVOCADOS

STUFFED BELL PEPPERS

STUFFED PORTOBELLO MUSHROOMS

LUNCH THREE STUFFED AMIGOS

Stuffed Avocados

Serves: 4 people · Total Time: 35 min

Ingredients

2 large avocados, halved & pitted
1 lb. ground turkey
1/2 yellow onion, diced
1 large zucchini, diced
1 c goat cheese, crumbled
1 tbsp cumin

1 tbsp garlic powder
2 tbsp paprika
1 tbsp chili powder
1/4 tsp cayenne pepper
Salt & pepper to taste
Olive oil

Method

1. Preheat the oven to 400 degrees.
2. Caramelize onions in a frying pan, add in diced zucchini. Season with salt and pepper. Transfer into a large mixing bowl.
3. Brown the turkey meat with cumin, garlic powder, paprika, chili powder, cayenne, salt and pepper.
4. Combine the meat, onion, and zucchini mixture in the mixing bowl. Once cooled, add goat cheese.
5. Scoop out some of the avocados to create a larger crater for stuffing, season the inside of avocados with salt and pepper. Add the scooped out avocado to the meat mixture. Season with salt and pepper to taste.
6. Generously stuff each half of the avocado. Bake in the oven uncovered for 20-25 minutes.
7. Serve with a side salad.

Stuffed Bell Peppers

Pair this dish with a side salad or a roasted vegetable to make it more of a meal. The leftovers pack well for lunch, so you may want to up the portion if you have children or a spouse who requires lunch the next day!

Serves: 2-4 people · Total Time: 50 min

Ingredients

2 large red bell peppers
1 lb. grass fed ground beef
1 c leftover brown rice
1/2 yellow onion, diced
1/2 c flat leaf parsley, chopped (set aside 2 tbsp for garnish)

4 cloves garlic, minced
1 c goat cheese, crumbled
1/2 tbsp cumin
1/2 tbsp smoked paprika
1/2 tbsp curry powder
Salt & pepper to taste

Method

1. Preheat the oven to 350 degrees.
2. Brown the onions in a frying pan on medium-high heat.
3. Add beef to brown first, then garlic and seasoning: cumin, smoked paprika, curry powder, salt and pepper.
4. Remove from the pan into a large mixing bowl to cool. Once cooled, add parsley, cheese, leftover rice, and more salt and pepper to taste. Mix well.
5. Cut the bell peppers in half, from stem to bottom. Remove the seeds. Stuff each half with the meat and rice mixture.
6. Lay stuffed bell peppers skin side down on a baking sheet. Cover with foil and bake for 25 minutes. Uncover and bake for 10 minutes.
7. Top with more fresh parsley.

Stuffed Portobello Mushrooms

Serves: 4 people · Total Time: 35 min

Ingredients

6 large portobello mushrooms
1/2 onion, diced
4 cloves of garlic, pressed
1 c quinoa
1 1/4 c broth

3 c pre-washed spinach
1/2 c tomatoes, diced
1 c goat cheese, crumbled
Salt & pepper to taste

Method

1. Preheat the oven to 400 degrees.
2. Stir fry onions and garlic in olive oil until fragrant.
3. Add quinoa, salt and pepper. Stir the quinoa to toast it until slightly brown.
4. Add the broth and bring to a boil. Cover and simmer on medium-low for 30 minutes.
5. When quinoa is done, fluff it with a fork and let it cool.
6. While quinoa is cooking, roast the mushrooms. Drizzle olive oil, salt and pepper on the inside of mushrooms. Lay them on a parchment lined baking sheet. Roast for approximately 20 minutes until mushrooms are cooked.
7. Remove quinoa from heat and fluff with a fork.
8. Fold in diced tomatoes and spinach until the spinach wilts.
9. Fill each mushroom with quinoa mixture, and top with goat cheese crumble. Serve with a side salad.

Pro Tip: When quinoa is fully cooked, it will expand and look more translucent.

Tacos

"It's okay if you fall apart sometimes. Tacos fall apart and we still love them."
— Anonymous

During the shutdown of 2020 I started to cook more than ever. This wasn't just because restaurants were no longer an option to dine with friends. I also had a perception shift that everything deserves to be celebrated with food. Short of Ground Hogs day, no day on the calendar escapes the appropriate food to celebrate it. Taco Tuesday was the consistent celebration that made weekdays more exciting. To keep Taco Tuesday fun, I created "Tacos Around The World" as a joke. My roommates at the time provided input on a country we wanted to visit, and I would research that country's cuisine and make it in the format of a handheld vessel. It was our way of traveling via our palette during the shutdown. Coincidentally, serving food in an edible vessel is practical and efficient, meeting the criteria of a great meal. Tacos aren't just for lunch or dinner, they are appropriate anytime of the day!

WAGYU BEEF
JAPANESE TERIYAKI SHRIMP
MISO GLAZED COD
POTATO LENTIL
SALMON
POLISH KIELBASA

CLASSIC TURKEY
WALNUT MEAT
PORTOBELLO MUSHROOM
ROASTED SWEET POTATO
LOW CARB GINGER SOY YELLOW TAIL
BEEF CHALUPA

TACOS

Wagyu Beef Tacos

Bon jour! This taco is inspired by the flavors in French cuisine, butter, truffle, and herbs de Provence. Wagyu beef has more marbling, resulting in a tender silky texture, a perfect choice for this bougie version of a beef taco.

Serves: 4 people · Total Time: 25 min

Ingredients

1 lb. ground wagyu beef
1 fennel bulb, thinly sliced
1/2 c parsley, chopped
2 tsp dried marjoram
2 tsp dried thyme
2 tsp dried rosemary
Truffle salt (or regular sea salt) & pepper
Butter (recommend using European butter for that added creaminess)
A squirt of lemon juice
Cooking sherry (or whiskey)
8 cactus tortillas (available in local Latino supermarkets or substitute with corn tortillas)
1 c goat cheese, crumbled
2 c microgreens
Chunky Salsa (see page 15 for recipe)

Method

1. Thinly slice fennel and sauté with butter, salt and pepper. Add a splash of cooking sherry (or whiskey), cover and simmer until a jam-like consistency. Remove from the pan, set aside.
2. In the same pan, brown the ground wagyu beef with butter, add marjoram, thyme, rosemary, truffle salt & pepper. When the beef is cooked, mix in half of the chopped parsley.
3. Warm up a stack of tortillas in a steamer. If you don't have a steamer, microwave the tortilla covered in a wet paper towel for 10 sec. 10 seconds longer if the tortilla is cold from the fridge.
4. Make the salsa.
5. Assemble the tacos: layer beef on the tortilla, add fennel next to the beef, top with micro greens, followed by salsa. Top with crumbled goat cheese.

Japanese Teriyaki Shrimp Tacos

We decided to travel to Japan for our Tacos Around The World. It is inspired by teriyaki bowls, simplifying all the components of a shrimp teriyaki bowl into a handheld format. On behalf of all Asians, I approve of ditching the chopsticks in this dish. Arigato!

Serves: 4 people · Total Time: 40 min

Ingredients

1 lb. deveined & shelled medium shrimp
2 c brown rice
2 c cooked, shelled edamame
1 pack of jicama wraps (8 ct)

Teriyaki sauce (see page 24 for recipe)
2 tbsp sesame oil, divide in 2
White sesame seeds, toasted
Furikake (seaweed seasoning)

Method

1. Cook the brown rice using a 1.25:1 ratio of water to rice, either on the stovetop ~30 minutes or in a steamer ~20 minutes..
2. While rice is cooking, make the teriyaki sauce.
3. Thaw and pat shrimp dry. Marinate in the teriyaki sauce for 15 minutes.
4. While the shrimp is marinating, warm through shelled edamame in a small pot, drizzle 1 tbsp sesame oil in the pot.
5. Saute the shrimp on high heat. They cook fast, and since Argentinian shrimp are pink when raw, check the firmness of the meat for doneness. About 5 minutes.
6. Toss cooked shrimp in more teriyaki sauce, remaining sesame oil, and sesame seeds.
7. Assemble tacos from the bottom up: starting with brown rice on jicama wrap, sprinkle furikake on the rice, and top with edamame and shrimp. Drizzle with teriyaki sauce.

Miso Glazed Cod Tacos

This recipe is a creative way to repurpose the miso glazed cod dish, if you have any left. On the off chance you are making this from the leftover miso glazed cod, no one will know it came from leftovers because it looks fancy and tastes amazing! Sshhh... it can be our best kept secret.

Serves: 4 people · Total Time: 35 min + 24 hours to marinate cod

Ingredients

4 cod fillets
2 c cooked, shelled edamame
Juice of a medium lemon
Avocado oil
1 pack of jicama wraps (8 ct)
2 cocktail or Persian cucumbers, thinly sliced diagonally
1 pack of seaweed snack
1 lemon, cut into 4 wedges

Miso Marinade

1/2 c white miso paste
1/2 c mirin
1/2 c sake
4 tbsp sugar

Method

1. Make the Miso Marinade (see page 33 for recipe)
2. Roast the Miso Glazed Cod (see page 131 for recipe)
3. Make the edamame puree by combining edamame, lemon juice, salt, and pepper in a food processor. Puree while adding avocado oil slowly until consistency is a smooth paste.
4. Assemble the taco from the bottom up: smear edamame puree on the jicama wrap, 3-4 thinly sliced cucumbers, then cod. Use a fork to break apart the fish into smaller pieces, making it easier to distribute across the taco.
5. Cut the seaweed snack into strips. Sprinkle on top of taco.

Vegan Potato Lentil Tacos

This traditional taco goes beyond the boundary of 60 minutes, but in Mexico time seems to stand still. It's a humble and hearty dish that is oh-so-satisfying! It reminds me to keep things simple and enjoy the process, in cooking and in life.

Serves: 4-6 people · Total Time: 65 min

Ingredients

1 1/2 lbs. baby gold potatoes
1 1/2 c green lentils
12 cactus tortilla (or corn tortilla)

Olive oil + coconut oil for frying
Salt & pepper to taste
Chunky Salsa (see page 15 for recipe)

Method

1. Preheat the oven to 400 degrees.
2. Cut the potatoes into bite-size pieces. Season with olive oil, salt and pepper. Roast with skin on for 20 minutes.
3. While the potatoes are roasting, cook the green lentils (see page 145 for recipe).
4. While the lentils are cooking, steam the tortilla from room temperature for 3-5 minutes. If you do not have a steamer, wrap the tortilla in a wet paper towel, and microwave for 15 seconds. Keep them warm, so they're pliable to fold without cracking.
5. When the potatoes are done and cooled, mash with a masher. Fold in the lentils. Taste the mixture at this point. Add more salt and pepper if needed.
6. Form the potato lentil mixture by hand into a small football-like shape. Place it in the center of a warm tortilla. Fold the tortilla into a half moon shape. Gently squeeze the filling to spread from the center toward the edge to seal the tortilla.
7. Heat to medium-high heat a frying pan of shallow oil. Fry the tacos 2 or 3 at a time, without crowding the pan. It should cause small bubbles. Fry for about 3 minutes per side or until golden brown.
8. Serve with salsa and hot sauce.

Salmon Tacos

Since Norway is famous for its salmon, we traveled to Norway for this taco. Unlike the instructions of a certain brand of Scandinavian furniture, the flavor is fresh and the execution is simple.

Serves: 4 people · Total Time: 25 min

Ingredients

4 sockeye salmon filets
1 lemon, sliced
2 packs of jicama wraps (8 ct)
8 taco tortillas
1 c radish, sliced
1 c cilantro, chopped

Sauce

1 1/2 c mayonnaise (or greek yogurt)
Juice of 2 lemons
4 cloves of garlic, pressed
Salt & pepper to taste

Method

1. Preheat the oven to 450 degrees.
2. Season salmon with salt and pepper, juice of 1/2 lemon, top each filet with 2 slices of lemon then roast in the oven for 12 minutes.
3. While the fish is roasting, slice the radish and chop the cilantro.
4. Make lemon garlic sauce: juice the lemons, press the garlic into a paste, and whisk all together with mayonnaise (or greek yogurt).
5. Assemble the tacos from the bottom: layer 2 jicama wraps edge to edge on top of the tortilla wrap, smear a layer of lemon garlic mayonnaise, followed by salmon, sliced radishes, then topped with cilantro.

Polish Kielbasa Tacos

The final stop of our Tacos Around The World We went to Poland. It's my version of a meat 'n potatoes meal. The potato sauce is velvety and tastes divine! It's a hearty dish that is fun to serve in an interactive style to a large group. Encourage everyone to assemble their own tacos.

Serves: 4 people · Total Time: 40 min

Ingredients

2 - 14 oz. Polish kielbasa
2 c shredded red cabbage
1 c apple cider vinegar
1/4 c honey
8 flour taco tortillas
Salt & pepper to taste

Potato Sauce

2 large red skin potatoes, diced
2 tbsp butter
6 cloves of garlic, pressed
Salt & pepper to taste
Hot water (as needed)

Method

1. First, braise cabbage in apple cider vinegar, honey, salt, and pepper for 30 minutes.
2. While braising is happening, boil and mash 2 large potatoes with butter, 6 large cloves of pressed garlic, salt, and pepper.
3. Add hot water to the mashed potatoes until a sauce-like consistency.
4. Score the kielbasa and pan fry the entire link. Once browned, slice kielbasa diagonally.
5. To assemble the tacos: layer bottom of tortilla with mashed potatoes, followed by sliced kielbasa, and top with braised cabbage.

TACOS AROUND THE WORLD

Classic Turkey Tacos

Sometimes after traveling the world, a classic dish is much welcomed. Enjoy this familiar dish with a slight twist with the pineapple salsa. Welcome home!

Serves: 4 people · Total Time: 30 min

Ingredients

1 1/2 lbs. organic ground turkey
1 bag of pre-washed shredded cabbage
2 tbsp garlic powder
2 tbsp cumin
2 tbsp paprika

1 lemon
2 avocados
8 flour taco tortillas
Salt & pepper to taste
Pineapple Salsa (see page 15 for recipe)

Method

1. Toss the cabbage with juice of half of a lemon, salt, and pepper. Set aside.
2. Brown the turkey seasoned with garlic powder, cumin, paprika, salt and pepper.
3. Make the salsa.
4. Assemble the taco from bottom up: on a tortilla layer the ground turkey, cabbage, sliced avocados. Top with salsa.

Vegan Walnut Meat Tacos

Close your eyes while eating this taco and you just might be convinced you are eating beef! Be generous with the seasoning and oil and toast the walnut meat until golden brown.

Serves: 4 people · Total Time: 35 min

Ingredients

3 c walnuts
1 tbsp garlic powder
1 tbsp cumin
2 tbsp paprika
1/2 tsp cayenne powder
1 tbsp tamari
Salt & pepper to taste
8 flour taco tortillas
Mango Salsa (see page 15 for recipe)

Guacamole

2 avocados
Pinch of salt
Pinch of garlic powder
1 tbsp lime or lemon juice

Method

1. Pulse whole walnuts in the food processor until they resemble the texture of ground meat.
2. Pan roast walnuts with olive oil, garlic powder, cumin, paprika, cayenne pepper, tamari, salt, and pepper. Stir fry walnuts until lightly browned.
3. To make the salsa: Dice the mango, onion, and serrano chili. Combine all ingredients with cilantro, lime juice, salt & pepper.
4. To make guacamole: Mash avocados, add garlic powder, lime juice, and salt. Mix well.
5. Assemble the taco from the bottom: start with guacamole, so walnuts have a landing place, walnuts, topped with salsa.

Variation: Instead of guacamole, use Cashew Sour Cream (see page 15 for recipe)

TACOS

Portobello Mushroom Tacos

This speedy dish is a lifesaver on those nights when you need dinner fast! It can be made vegan by omitting the goat cheese. It looks healthy and tastes fresh and is easy to clean up. You're welcome.

Serves: 4 people · Total Time: 30 min

Ingredients

6 large portobello mushrooms
7 oz. baby arugula, pre-washed
1 pack of jicama wraps (8 ct)
4 tbsp dairy free pesto (see page 13 for recipe)
2 tbsp extra virgin olive oil
Garlic powder
Salt & pepper
4 tbsp goat cheese, crumbled
2 tbsp sunflower seeds

Method

1. Preheat the oven to 400 degrees.
2. Season the portobello mushrooms whole with olive oil, salt, pepper, and garlic powder. Roast for 20 minutes.
3. Once the mushrooms are cooled, slice diagonally to create a wider surface area.
4. Whisk pesto with olive oil, salt & pepper to a dressing-like consistency. Toss arugula in it.
5. Assemble the taco from the bottom: layer sliced mushrooms on a jicama wrap, followed by arugula, goat cheese, and sunflower seeds.

Vegan Sweet Potato Tacos

Serves: 4 people · Total Time: 35 min

Ingredients

4 medium size sweet potatoes, diced
1 red bell pepper
1 onion
2 c walnut pieces
1 pack jicama wraps (8 ct)
1/2 c cilantro
Salt & pepper to taste
Olive oil

Sauce

1 tsp dried oregano
1/2 c vegan mayo
Juice of a small lemon

Taco Seasoning (divide into 2 portions)

1 tbsp cumin
2 tbsp paprika
1 tbsp garlic powder
1/4 tsp cayenne pepper
Salt & pepper

Method

1. Preheat the oven to 425 degrees.
2. Season diced sweet potatoes with taco seasoning. Roast for 30 minutes until golden. Flip the sweet potatoes halfway through cooking.
3. While the potatoes are roasting, caramelize onions and bell peppers with salt and pepper in a frying pan. Set aside.
4. In the same pan, stir fry the walnut pieces with olive oil, and taco seasoning until lightly brown.
5. Make the sauce: whisk together vegan mayo, lemon juice, and oregano.
6. Assemble the taco from the bottom: place roasted potatoes on a jicama wrap, followed by onions, bell peppers, and toasted walnuts. Drizzle sauce, then garnish with fresh cilantro.

TACOS

Low Carb Ginger Soy Yellowtail Fish Tacos

Serves: 3 people · Total Time: 25 min + 20 min or overnight to marinate fish

Ingredients

6 yellowtail loins
1 12 oz. sesame Asian crunch salad kit
3 stalks of scallions, chopped
1 pack of Folio cheese wrap (8 ct)
Ponzu cream (see page 16 for recipe)
Chili oil (optional)

Ginger Soy Marinade

1/2 c low sodium soy sauce
1/4 c rice wine vinegar
2 tbsp grated ginger root

Method

1. Preheat the oven to 420 degrees.
2. Rinse and pat dry each fish loin. Marinate in ginger soy marinade for at least 20 minutes or overnight.
3. Roast fish for 15 min.
4. Assemble salad in a large bowl. Set aside.
5. Make ponzu cream as directed. Optional: add a few dashes of chili oil to spice up ponzu cream.
6. Use Folio wrap at room temperature by leaving it out of the fridge for 20 minutes. Texture will become similar to a tortilla wrap.
7. Assemble the taco from the bottom: on a cheese wrap, layer the salad first, followed by flaked fish. Drizzle ponzu cream and sprinkle chopped scallions.

Beef Chalupas

Serves: 4 people · Total Time: 35 min + 10 min or overnight for pickling

Ingredients

2 lbs. grass fed ground beef
2 avocados, sliced
2 c shredded cabbage (pre-shredded)
2 c shredded carrots (pre-shredded)
4 cocktail or Persian cucumbers, sliced
1/2 red onion, thinly sliced
Sherry vinegar (or white vinegar)
3 tbsp sea salt
8 flour taco tortillas
2 packs of jicama wrap (16 ct)

Taco Seasoning

2 tbsp cumin
3 tbsp garlic powder
1 tbsp oregano
1/2 tsp cayenne pepper
Salt & pepper

Sauce

1/2 c mayonnaise
1 tbsp horseradish
Juice of a lemon
Salt & pepper

Method

1. Pickle onions in sherry vinegar or any white vinegar for a minimum of 30 minutes, or overnight. This is a drive-by, accelerated pickling. Here's how:
   - Douse sliced onions with 3 tbsp salt, use your hands to lightly massage the onions with salt. Let sit for 10 minutes.
   - Rinse the onion salt mixture with cold water.
   - In a mason jar, add enough vinegar to cover the sliced onions.
2. Toss shredded cabbage, shredded carrots, and chopped scallions in fresh lemon juice, salt, and pepper at least 30 minutes before serving
3. Season and brown the ground beef with taco seasoning.
4. Make the sauce: combine mayo, horseradish, lemon juice, salt & pepper to taste.
5. Assemble the tacos from the bottom: layer 2 jicama wraps edge to edge on top of a flour tortilla. Add beef, followed by cabbage/ carrots, cucumbers, avocados, then pickled onions.

Dinner

"After a good dinner, one can forgive anybody, even one's own relations."
— Oscar Wilde

DINNER

MAIN DISHES
VEGAN BOWLS

Dinner: Main Dishes

"The main thing is to keep the main thing the main thing."
– Stephen Covey, The Seven Habits of Highly Effective People

I'm a grazer, someone who likes to turn side dishes into a meal, but I have to remember there are other people in my life who would agree with Stephen Covey. The look of panic in my husband's eyes when I just cook tapas style is a confirmation I need to remember what the main thing is.

MISO GLAZED COD

MEDITERRANEAN STYLE MAHI MAHI

MAPO TOFU

POKE BOWL

CHICKEN PUMPKIN CURRY

DINNER: MAIN DISHES

MAPO TOFU

Miso Glazed Cod

A Nobu-inspired dish. It tastes expensive too! Serve this dish at a dinner party to impress and love on your guests. If the fish still tastes fishy, a squirt of lemon juice will remedy that.

Serves: 4 people · Total Time: 25 min + 24 hours to marinate fish

Ingredients

4 cod fillets
Miso Marinade (see page 33 for recipe)
1 lemon, cut into 4 wedges

Method

1. Preheat the oven to 400 degrees.
2. Prepare the miso marinade: combine mirin, sake, and sugar in a sauce pot and bring to a boil for 20 seconds to cook off the alcohol. Remove from heat, and whisk in white miso paste until smooth.
3. Slather the marinade on the fish. Refrigerate up to 2 days, or at a minimum 24 hours.
4. Place a parchment lined baking sheet in the oven to warm up the baking sheet.
5. Wipe off excess marinade, leaving a thin layer on the fish. Pan fry the fish 2-3 minutes per side to caramelize the outside, then transfer onto the warmed baking sheet. Bake for 5-10 minutes.
6. Serve with forbidden black rice, and garlic bok choy.

2 for 1 Meal Idea: Turn this dish into a taco! (see page 107 for recipe)

Mediterranean Style Mahi Mahi

This is one of our household favorite weeknight dishes. It is fast, flavorful, and easy to clean up. If you want to eliminate washing dishes altogether, just eat off of the baking sheet. Call it communal dining. No shame.

Serves: 6 people · Total Time: 25 min

Ingredients

6 mahi mahi filets
1/3 c kalamata olives, rough chopped
1/3 c sundried tomatoes, rough chopped
5 cloves of garlic, pressed
1/2 c of cilantro, chopped
Zest of 2 lemons
Juice of 1 lemon

Method

1. Preheat the oven to 400 degrees.
2. Pat dry filets and lay on a parchment lined baking sheet.
3. Combine lemon zest, garlic, and 3 tbsp olive oil, salt & pepper. Cover both sides of each filet with the marinade. Roast for 12-15 minutes.
4. In the meantime, combine the olives and sundried tomatoes. Top each filet with the olives/ sundried tomato mixture when cooked. Sprinkle cilantro and more lemon zest.
5. Serve over herbed (roughly chopped fresh parsley or cilantro) brown rice and roasted vegetables.

DINNER: MAIN DISHES

Mapo Tofu

This dish is another comfort food for me. It is a flavor bomb too! Serve it over a bowl of steaming rice or porridge to complement the salty, complex flavor. It can be made vegetarian by omitting the pork.

Serves: 4 people · Total Time: 25 min

Ingredients

1/2 lb. ground pork
1 block of medium or soft tofu
1 bunch of enoki mushrooms, chopped
3 large cloves of garlic, minced
2 tbsp fresh ginger root, chopped
3 stalks of scallions, chopped
1 red chili pepper, finely chopped & de-seed
2 tbsp oyster sauce

2 tbsp sesame oil
1 tbsp spicy bean paste (or adjust to your spice level)
1/2 tbsp chili oil (or adjust to your spice level)
1/2 tbsp dark vinegar
1/2 c water
1 tsp sugar
White pepper to taste

Method

1. Pan fry garlic, ginger, and the white part of the scallions with sesame oil until fragrant.
2. Brown the pork seasoned with white pepper. Add spicy bean paste, oyster sauce, sugar, and some water.
3. Add the enoki mushrooms, stir to break up the pieces. Lower the heat to medium. The mushrooms act as a thickening agent, so heat through until the sauce thickens.
4. Add the tofu. Gently fold them into the sauce without breaking.
5. Taste, then add more water if needed. Cover with lid and let simmer until large bubbles appear and sauce thickens.
6. Add chili, the green part of scallions, vinegar, and chili oil. Gently fold all ingredients until well incorporated.
7. Serve over brown or white rice.

Poke Bowl

Poke means chopped, not necessarily raw seafood, so those who choose not to consume raw food, can enjoy the cooked shrimp option. The dish can be served buffet style, so everyone can customize their own bowls. It is also a great idea for a casual dinner party!

Serves: 4 people · Total Time: 30 min
+ 24 hours to marinate tuna or +15 min to marinate shrimp

Ingredients

1 lb shrimp or 2 c cubed sushi grade ahi tuna
2 large avocados
2 c cooked, shelled edamame
1/2 c cocktail or Persian cucumbers, sliced
1/2 c Japanese red pickled radish (sold as a condiment for curry dishes in most Japanese supermarkets like Marukai, Nijiya, or Mitsuwa. Omit if you do not have a Japanese market near you)
1/2 c pickled ginger slices

2 c brown or white rice
2 c power greens salad
Furikake (seaweed seasoning)
Chipotle mayo (any brand)

Poke Marinade

1/2 c ponzu sauce
1/2 c soy sauce
1/4 c sesame oil

Method: Shrimp Poke Bowl

1. Thaw, rinse, and pat shrimp dry. Marinate in ponzu, soy sauce, and sesame oil for 15 minutes.
2. In a large bowl, combine ponzu, soy, and sesame oil. Set aside.
3. Stir fry the shrimp with 1 tbsp of sesame oil at medium-high heat. When the texture firms up, shrimp is cooked. Remove promptly and transfer into the large bowl.

Method: Tuna Poke Bowl

1. Toss the fresh, sushi grade tuna chunks into the large bowl to coat evenly. Cover, and store in the fridge overnight.

Assemble either bowl: put a base layer of white or brown rice (serve half rice/half power greens salad for a lower carb option), top with shrimp or tuna. Then create zones around your protein. Add sliced cucumbers, pickled red radish, ginger, edamame, and avocado slices. Drizzle chipotle mayo and sprinkle it with furikake.

DINNER: MAIN DISHES

Chicken Pumpkin Curry

Serves: 4 people · Total Time: 50 min

Ingredients

3 organic chicken breasts, diced into large chunks
1 c sugar snap peas or snow peas
2 medium carrots, sliced into 1/8" diagonal discs
1 red bell peppers, diced
1/2 yellow onion, diced
1/4 c fresh ginger root, sliced into discs
5 cloves of garlic, minced

1 can of pumpkin puree
1 can of full-fat coconut milk
Organic vegetable broth (as needed)
4 tbsp yellow curry powder
1 tbsp cumin
1/2 tbsp cinnamon
1/2 tbsp paprika
Salt & pepper to taste
Coconut oil

Method

1. Dice chicken into bite sized chunks. Marinate in half a can of coconut milk, 2 tbsp curry powder, salt, and pepper for a minimum of 20 minutes.
2. Add 2 tbsp of coconut oil to a saute pan, brown the chicken on all sides. Remove from the pan.
3. Add more coconut oil as needed. In the same pan, saute ginger until fragrant, add the onion to brown, then add chopped garlic. Stir fry on medium-high heat.
4. Add carrots next, saute for 3 minutes. Followed by snap peas and bell peppers. Season with salt and pepper.
5. Turn the heat to high. Add the chicken back into the pan, followed by the rest of the coconut milk, pumpkin puree, and enough broth to cover the vegetables and chicken.
6. Add the remaining curry powder and all seasoning. Bring the broth to a gentle boil. Turn the heat to low. Cover and simmer for 30 minutes.
7. Serve over cauliflower rice, brown or white rice.

Dinner: Vegan Bowls

This is a superfoods section. Each ingredient is not only good for you, but together, they also create a flavor-packed meal that is versatile, customizable, and efficient to make. Most of them can be made ahead of time and eaten through the week in different ways, making them feel and look like a new dish with each combination. Enclosed are sample bowls to get your creative juices flowing. Let your creativity go wild!

BASES: GRAINS & LEGUMES

TOPPINGS: COOKED & RAW

MY GO-TO BOWLS

DINNER: VEGAN BOWLS

Vegan Bowls: Bases

Grains are like the ambassadors of the food world — they are accessible to most people. For some, it is comfort food, to others it is the only source of sustenance. For busy people, it is a life saver. Enjoy these simple combinations as a stand alone dish or pair with the toppings and sauces for a complete vegan bowl experience.

BASES:

GRAINS & LEGUMES

DINNER: VEGAN BOWL BASES

Pesto Quinoa

Add this pesto quinoa to any salad for a vegetarian protein option, or top with some avocados to consume as a stand alone meal.

Serves: 2-3 people · Total Time: 30 min

Ingredients

2 tbsp dairy free pesto (see page 13 for recipe)
1 c tricolor quinoa
1 1/2 c broth
1/2 red bell pepper, diced
1/2 yellow or orange bell peppers, diced
3 cloves of fresh garlic, crushed
2 tbsp extra virgin olive oil
Salt & pepper to taste

Pro Tip: When quinoa is fully cooked, it will expand and look more translucent.

Method

1. Add olive oil to the pot to toast the quinoa at medium-high heat.
2. Add broth, salt, and pepper, and bring to a boil. Cover and simmer on medium-low heat for 30 minutes.
3. When quinoa is done, fluff it with a fork.
4. Add freshly crushed garlic, diced bell peppers, and pesto while quinoa is warm.
5. Store overnight to allow flavors to fully incorporate.

Mediterranean Quinoa

Serves: 4 people · Total Time: 35 min

Ingredients

2 c tri-color quinoa
1/2 onion, diced
1/2 red bell pepper, diced
1/2 yellow or orange bell pepper, diced
2 1/2 c vegetable broth
1/3 c kalamata olives, pitted, whole
1/3 c Persian cucumbers, diced
1 tbsp chopped or julienned sun-dried tomatoes
2 tbsp capers

Pro Tip: When quinoa is fully cooked, it will expand and look more translucent.

Method

1. Add olive oil to the pot, saute chopped onions, then toast the quinoa at medium-high heat.
2. Add broth, salt, and pepper, and turn up the heat to bring to a boil. Then cover and simmer on medium-low for 30 minutes.
3. When quinoa is done, fluff it with a fork and let it cool.
4. Add bell peppers, sun-dried tomatoes, capers, olives, and cucumbers to quinoa.
5. Serve with crumbled goat cheese on top (optional).

Green Lentil & Farro

Serves: 4 people · **Total Time: 40 min using Instapot or 50 min stovetop**

Ingredients

2 c green lentils
1 c farro
3 1/2 c vegetable broth
2 tbsp extra virgin olive oil
Pinch of salt & pepper

Method

1. Farro will take the longest to cook, prioritize this step. Combine farro with 1 1/2 cup of vegetable broth in Instapot, select "Grains" setting, 40 minutes. If you don't have an Instapot, simmer in a covered pot on the stove for 50 minutes. Farro will look fluffy almost like brown rice when done.
2. In a separate pot, toast the green lentils in olive oil for 3 minutes.
3. Add the remaining broth, salt, and pepper. Bring to a boil, then cover and simmer for 15-20 minutes depending on how soft you like your lentils. 15 minutes will be more al dente.
4. Combine the lentils and farro together for a hearty, fiber and protein rich dish.

Rice & Black Beans

A classic, and a canvas for you to create. I appreciate this simple and nutritious option by itself or as part of a meal. Did you know rice and beans together make a complete protein? A big promise for such a humble dish.

Serves: 4-6 people · **Total Time: 25 min using rice cooker or 35 min stovetop**

Ingredients

1/2 onion
4 cloves of garlic
2 c multi-grain rice or brown rice
2 1/4 c chicken or vegetable broth
1 can of black beans, drained and rinsed
Salt & pepper to taste
2 tbsp extra virgin olive oil

Method

1. Add brown rice, broth, onion, and garlic in a rice cooker and cook for 20 minutes. If using the traditional stove top method, bring the broth to a boil on high heat, then cover and lower heat to medium-low to simmer for 30 minutes.
2. Add in black beans when rice is done, season with salt and pepper, and a drizzle of olive oil.

Forbidden Rice

Forbidden rice, or black rice, stands out from other rice as it is higher in protein, and lower in calories and carbohydrates. It is also packed with fiber and mineral content. It is so superior that in ancient China it was reserved exclusively for the Emperor and royalty, hence the name, forbidden. I love serving the savory option of this rice with curry.

Serves: 2 people · Total Time: 40 min

Savory

Ingredients

1 c forbidden or black rice
1 1/4 c full-fat coconut milk
1 c water

Method

1. Combine rice and coconut milk in a pot. Bring to a boil on high heat, then cover and simmer on medium-low heat for 30-35 minutes.
2. Best served with Miso Glazed Cod, or with a curry dish.

Sweet

Ingredients

1 c forbidden or black rice
1 1/4 c full-fat coconut milk
1 c water
2 tbsp sugar
1/4 c condensed milk
2 fresh mangos, sliced

Method

1. Combine rice, coconut milk, and sugar in a pot. Bring to a boil on high heat, then cover and simmer on medium-low heat for 30-35 minutes.
2. Once the rice is cooled. Top with fresh mangoes and drizzle with condensed milk.

Vegan Bowls: Toppings

Your oven and Instapot will be your best friend in this section. Prepare these toppings ahead of time to top your bowls and choose your sauces from the Sauces, Dressings & Marinades section.

TOPPINGS:

COOKED & RAW

DINNER: VEGAN BOWL TOPPINGS

Roasted Vegetables

All vegetables take a similar amount of time to roast. Shop and cook what's in season or choose 3 or 4 of your favorites from the list below. Create your own bowl or see *My Go-To Bowls* for ideas.

Each vegetable is approximately 4 servings · Total Time: 25 min each

Ingredients

4 c broccoli
4 c cauliflower
3 c golden beets, cubed (roast with skin on)
3 c sweet potatoes, cubed (peel skin first)
3 c crimini mushrooms, halved (wipe off dirt with a damp towel)
3 c red bell peppers, cubed
3 c carrots, sliced 1/4 inch discs

Method

1. Preheat oven to 425 degrees.
2. Roast them individually on separate baking sheets. Or, half the amount to roast on the same sheet.
3. Space out the vegetables on a parchment lined baking sheet for even roasting.
4. Olive oil and salt the vegetables, toss to mix evenly.
5. Roast for 15-20 minutes until vegetables are golden brown. Check and flip the vegetables after 10 minutes.

Pressure Cooked Chickpeas

Serves: 6-8 people · Total Time: 30 min

Ingredients

2 c chickpeas, soaked overnight
1 can of diced tomatoes
1/2 onion, diced
4 cloves of garlic, minced
1 bay leaf
2 tsp salt
Enough water to cover all ingredients

Method

1. Combine all ingredients in the Instapot and pressure cook on high for 25 minutes.
2. Either manually release or let the Instapot naturally release the pressure. Serve as is.

Optional Method

1. If you don't have an Instapot, fret not. You can cook chickpeas in a crockpot on high setting for 2-3 hours.

Raw Toppings

Shop for what's in season or choose a few of your favorites from the list below to complement the cooked toppings.

Each vegetable is approximately 4 servings · Total Time: 5 min each

Ingredients

2 c firm tofu, cubed
2 c cherry tomatoes, halved
2 c sugar snap peas, sliced at a diagonal to 1/4 inch chunks
2 medium avocados, sliced
2 c radishes, thinly sliced

DINNER: VEGAN BOWL TOPPINGS

Vegan Bowls: My Go-To's

There are so many combinations you can make in this Vegan Bowl section. Listed below are three of my favorites, my go-to bowls. Feel free to create your own combinations. If you don't know where to begin, ask yourself how much time do you have? Start with the recipe that fits your time frame, choosing a base you want, then the toppings. Finally, choose your sauce to tie all the flavors together.

THE GREEN BOWL

THE ROYAL BOWL

THE SOUTHWESTERN BOWL

DINNER: MY GO-TO VEGAN BOWLS

The Green Bowl

I love this bowl. It is a vision of health. The combination is satiating with fiber, good fat, and both sauce options pack in a lot of flavor!

Serves: 1 person · Total Time: 40 min

Base   Green Lentils & Farro

Toppings   Roasted Broccoli
                      Radishes
                      Avocados
                      Sugar Snap Peas

Sauce   Ponzu Cream (photographed, see page 16 for recipe) or
                      Garlic Tahini (see page 20 for recipe)

The Royal Bowl

This is a great starter bowl for anyone who has reservations about vegetables. It is a bit on the sweet side with a sesame peanut sauce, but like a great PB & J sandwich, who does not like a touch of peanut butter sweetness?!

Serves: 1 person · Total Time: 40 min

Base	Savory Forbidden Rice
Toppings	Roasted Golden Beets Roasted Broccoli Roasted Carrots Tofu
Sauce	Sesame Peanut (photographed, see page 28 for recipe) or Turmeric Miso (see page 27 for recipe)

The Southwestern Bowl

This colorful bowl features some familiar ingredients and flavors. It is like eating a meal at grandma's house, comforting and filling and sure to please.

Serves: 1 person · Total Time: 40 min

Base	Rice & Black Beans
Toppings	Roasted Sweet Potatoes Roasted Cauliflowers Radishes Avocados Cherry Tomatoes Cilantro, chopped (optional)
Sauce	Cashew Sour Cream (see page 15 for recipe)

DINNER: MY GO-TO VEGAN BOWLS

Closing

As diverse as cuisines are, so are our experiences and stories surrounding the food we love. Whether cooking meals has been a burden for you because of resource scarcity or of technical challenges, I hope the simplicity and diversity of the recipes in this cookbook have empowered you to try something new.

Letting go of the pasts that may be holding us back from living our lives to the fullest is just a first step. The redemption from my childhood paved a way for me to own cooking as my creative outlet, one that anchors me to my authentic self and to those I love and to new relationships I look forward to forming.

My ultimate hope is that you will let food anchor you in your busy life by fueling you with the nutrition and energy to do what you are called to do. Let it anchor you to a community, full of rich and meaningful relationships. By sharing meals may you feed those relationships and by extension your soul as you traverse through the twists and turns in life.

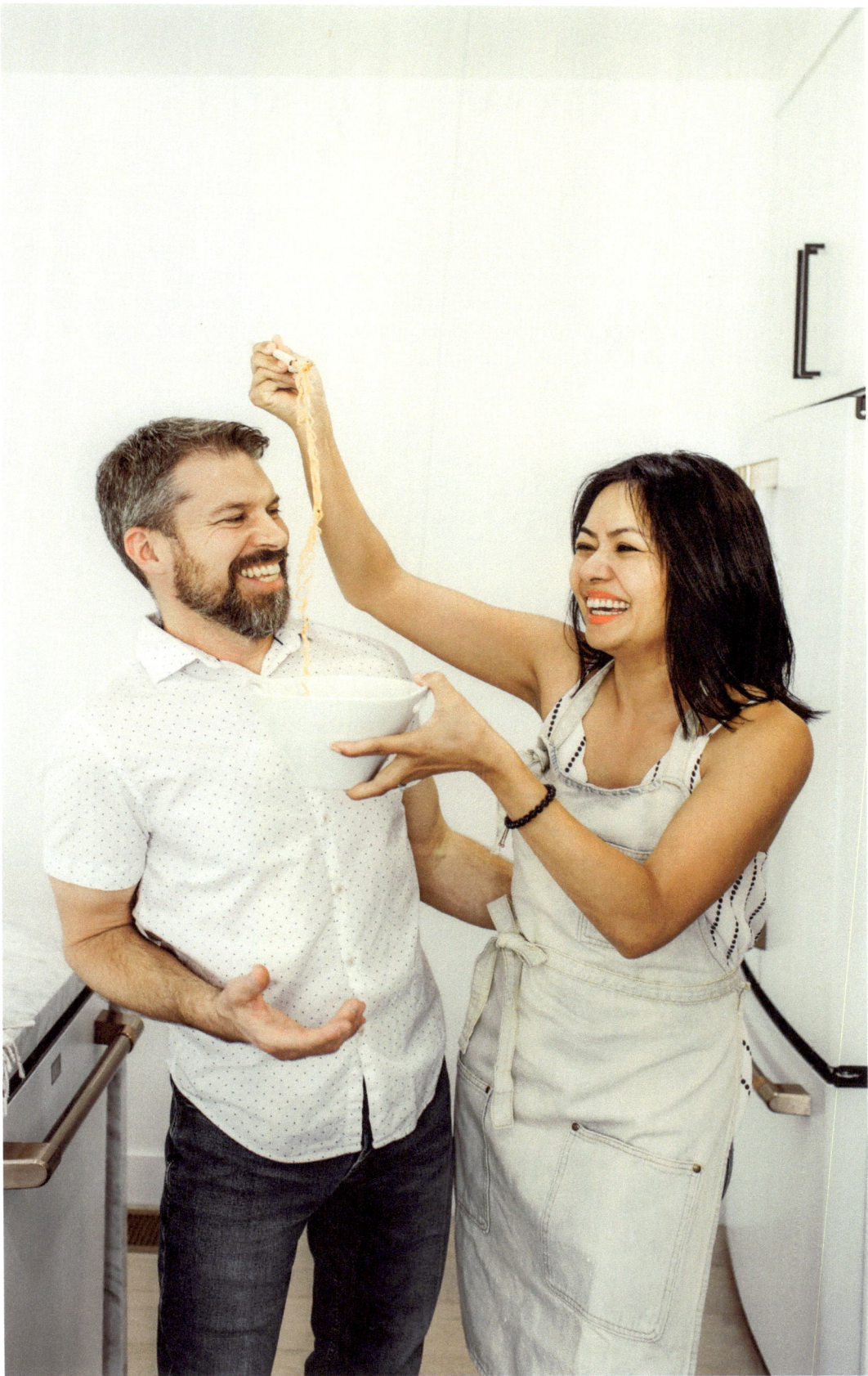

Acknowledgments

A single ingredient can inspire an orgasmic culinary experience. Together, multiple individual ingredients can turn that experience into an unforgettable meal. Writing Food That Anchors has been an unforgettable journey made possible by Jesus, who ordained the village of individuals, and provided the resources to bring this assignment into reality. I'm grateful to you all. This book is for His glory!

TO MY FAMILY & FRIENDS:

To my adventurous Dad: Thank you for instilling in me an appreciation for all foods. You taught me everything is worth a try and if I did not like something to just eat less of it.

To my talented Mom: Thank you for teaching me creative ways to cook, ways to make a dish healthier without sacrificing flavors. Your palette to discern every ingredient in a dish is an inspiration!

To my beautiful sister, Megan: Thank you for showing me a fancy way to make ramen. Who knew that bowl would ignite my love for cooking?! You are also a real food adventurer. You know and appreciate good food no matter where or how it is served.

To my mighty husband, Alex: Thank you for being my guinea pig and being my biggest fan. Without your bottomless appetite, these recipes would be more challenging to develop. I love you!

To my beta readers, Alexa, Arianna, Chrissy, Julianna: Thank you for extracting the gold in this book and believing in the heart behind it. It literally would read like a book of fortune cookie inserts without your input!

To my amazing tribe: Thank you for running this marathon with me. You provided the hydration, and ran the race with me. Thank you for allowing me to raid your homes for decorations & props, allowing me to feed you, for liking my countless food photos, and for believing in me.

To my guardian angels, John, Linda, Corey: Thank you for your generosity, patience, and counsel. Your integrity shines like a beacon of hope in an endangered world.

Community

Thank you for reading Food That Anchors!

Beyond these recipes, Food That Anchors is a community. Please share your feedback or photos of recipes you cooked on social media and tag us using **@foodthatanchors.**

Did this cookbook help you in some way? If so, I'd love to hear about it. Please consider writing a review with your honest impressions on Amazon, Goodreads, or the platform of your choosing. Your feedback is incredibly valuable in helping readers find the right cookbook for their needs.

For free monthly meal plans including grocery links, video recipes and additional resources, scan the QR code below.

Happy Cooking,

Ellen

References

(1) Bourdain, Anthony. Kitchen Confidential: Adventures in the Culinary Underbelly. Unabridged. New York: Random House, 2000.

(2) 16 of the Best Peter the Great Quotes. Quoteikon. https://www.quoteikon.com/peter-the-great-quotes.html, June 1, 2022.

(3) Wilde, Oscar, and Charles Shannon. A Woman of No Importance. London: John Lane at the sign of the Bodley Head in Vigo Street, 1894.

FOOD THAT ANCHORS
Copyright © 2022 by Ellen C Lee

All rights reserved. No portion of this book may be reproduced – mechanically, electronically, or by any other means, including photocopying – without written permission of the publisher.

ISBN 979-8-9866874-0-7
Ebook 979-8-9866874-1-4

Cover & Layout Designer: Faith Bretow, Wilde Faith Creative, hello@wildefaith.com
Editors: Alyssa Jenkins & Alyx Barbeau, Kingdom Books Publishing, info@kingdombookpublishing.com
Food Photographer: Arianna Negri, Sunflower Creative Co., arianna@sunflowercreativeco.com
Lifestyle Photographer: Whitney Parker, Paco and Betty, pb@pacoandbetty.com

First print edition 2022.

Published by Ellen C Lee.

Connect with Ellen online:
Website: foodthatanchors.com
Email: hello@foodthatanchors.com
Instagram, Pinterest, YouTube, Facebook: @foodthatanchors

www.ingramcontent.com/pod-product-compliance
Lightning Source LLC
Chambersburg PA
CBHW041423010526
44119CB00015B/348